KU-216-533

Sunset at Botallack

CORNWALL'S FAR WEST

St. Ives, Mount's Bay and the Land's End Peninsula

A pictorial souvenir

SALMON

INTRODUCTION

One of the most fascinating parts of the British Isles, Cornwall is a peninsula with its own traditions, language and legends. The far west of the county offers an atmospheric landscape which combines spectacular cliff scenery with secluded coves of golden sand. The coastline is one of the most spectacular anywhere in Britain, stretching from St. Ives in the north with its fine beaches around the rugged cliff scenery of Land's End, to the wide sweep of Mount's Bay. The peninsula is rich in history with the remains of Iron Age villages, burial chambers and standing stones scattered across the moorland, revealing something of the life of our Celtic ancestors. The rich seams of the far west have been mined since Stone Age times, but it was in the 19th century that the mining of copper and tin reached its zenith, leaving a legacy of abandoned engine houses, an evocative reminder of an industry now completely lost. In contrast, winding country lanes are bordered by ancient hedges where wild flowers grow in profusion, and the offshore stacks and jagged cliff ledges around the coast provide nesting sites for a wide variety of sea-birds. Favoured by the Gulf Stream and a warm, damp climate, subtropical trees and shrubs grow in profusion in parks and gardens. Artists have always been attracted to Cornwall's picturesque old fishing villages, and St. Ives and Newlyn have long nurtured vibrant artistic communities.

Mount's Bay

MOUNT'S BAY

The wide curve of Mount's Bay offers spectacular views west towards the Land's End Peninsula and east towards the Lizard. A large part of the bay was originally marshy woodland which was submerged in prehistoric times, giving rise to the legend of the Lost Land of Lyonesse which features in the Arthurian stories. Until the development of Penzance, Marazion was the main trading port on Mount's Bay, but today it is known chiefly as the nearest point on the mainland to the rocky pyramid of St. Michael's Mount. Rising nearly 300 feet from the sea, it can be reached from the mainland by a ferry or, at low tide, along a stone causeway. This romantic and beautiful little island was originally the site of a Benedictine priory established by Edward the Confessor, but is now topped by a spectacular medieval castle and church. St. Michael's Mount is thought to have been the site of a port exporting tin in the late Iron Age and the little harbour is still busy with small craft of all kinds. England's most westerly town, Penzance was once a major West Country port and the harbour is still a bustling centre of activity used mainly by private craft, but also by the ferry which plies between the mainland and the Isles of Scilly. Westwards from Penzance is the old fishing village of Newlyn. An artists' colony

6 St. Michael's Mount

St. Michael's Mount

Subtropical plants flourish at Trengwainton Garden

was established here in 1883 and Newlyn is still famed as a centre for artists. To the east, secluded Prussia Cove is one of several attractive coves which line the rocky shore of the bay. High on the cliffs above beautiful little Rinsey Cove, not far from the popular beach at Praa Sands, is the engine house of Wheal Prosper Mine, also known as Rinsey Mine, a dramatic reminder of the local mining heritage. With one of the mildest climates in Britain, the area around Mount's Bay is rich in glorious gardens where exotic plants flourish. Trengwainton Garden near Penzance contains many species which are not grown in the open anywhere else in the country. South of Penzance, the fine house at Trereife is set in sweeping landscaped parkland with woodland walks, whilst nearby Trewidden, one of the finest informal gardens in the south-west of England, was established in the late 1880s and now boasts one of the largest selections of camellias in the country as well as an outstanding collection of tree ferns.

Rinsey Mine

10 At Praa Sands there is a mile-long stretch of beach

Prussia Cove was the haunt of John Carter, a notorious smuggler known as the "King of Prussia"

St. Michael's Mount

A causeway connects St. Michael's Mount to the mainland at low tide

14 Evening sunshine at Penzance harbour

Consecrated in 1836, St. Mary's Church in Penzance overlooks the town's harbour

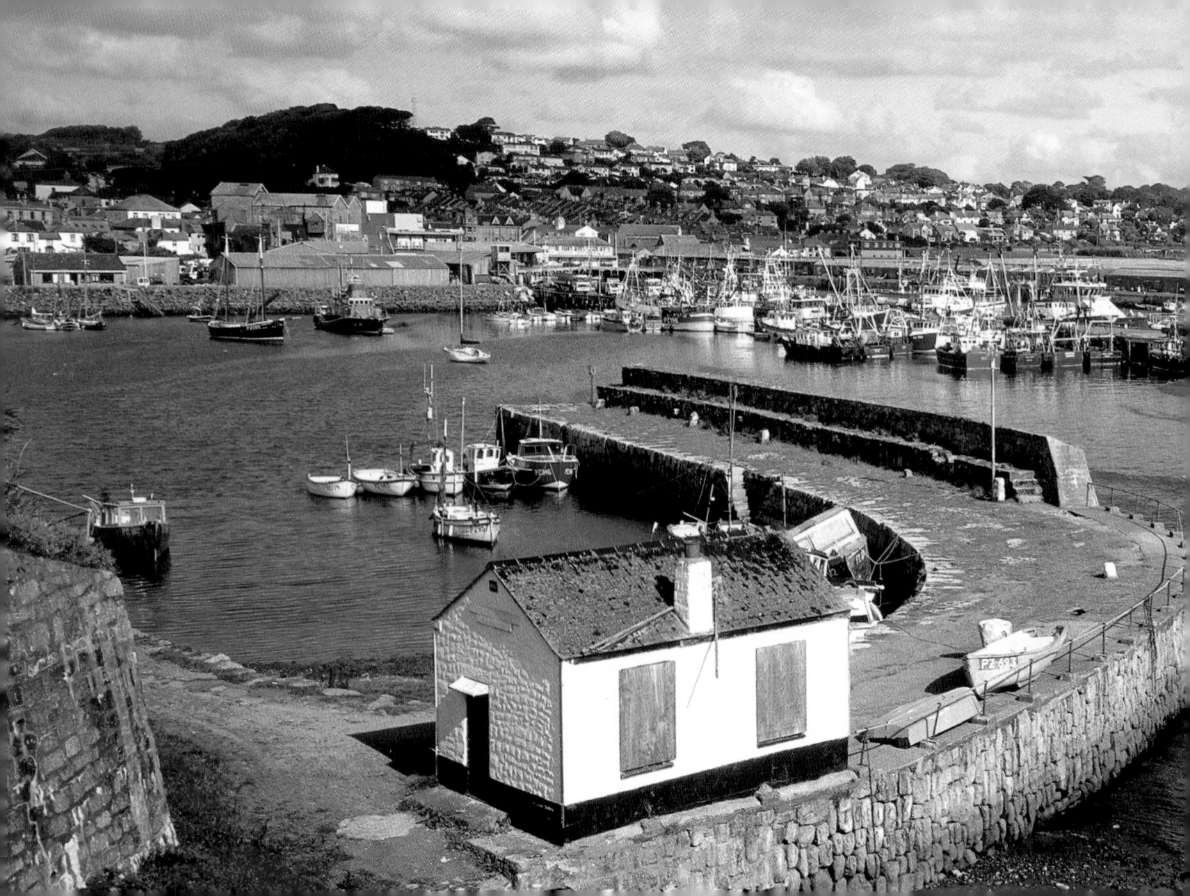
PZ

Newlyn is Cornwall's premier fishing port

18 Trereife House and garden are set in beautiful parkland at the head of the Newlyn Valley

This red telephone box is an unusual feature of Trewidden Gardens, near Penzance

LAND'S END PENINSULA

The impressive granite cliffs at Land's End, England's most westerly mainland point, are battered relentlessly by Atlantic waves and gales. The 200-feet-high cliffs are all that now remain of a vast mountain chain that once extended from the Isles of Scilly through Cornwall and on to Brittany. The Longships Lighthouse stands more than a mile out to sea, warning shipping away from this treacherous stretch of the coast. At one end of the magnificent sweep of nearby Whitesand Bay is Sennen Cove, where the Atlantic rollers pound onto the beach, creating ideal conditions for surfers. The little harbour, with its narrow quay, houses the lifeboat which serves wild Land's End with its treacherous currents and offshore rock stacks. Situated in an area of stunning coastal scenery, several promontories jut out from Cornwall's north coast, including Cape Cornwall, once a centre for tin mining, Pendeen Watch, where a lighthouse has guided shipping for over one hundred years, and Gurnards Head, with its prehistoric fort. The village of Zennor lies on a coastal plateau which has been cultivated since the Iron Age. The 12th century church is dedicated to the little known St. Senara, believed to have been a Breton princess who was miraculously saved from drowning. In the 19th century the far west of Cornwall was the centre of an extensive tin and copper mining industry. Monuments to this

 Sennen Cove

Land's End

22 Rough seas at Cape Cornwall

heritage, both Botallack and the Levant Mines were famous for their rich deposits of ore which were mined far out under the sea. This area is also known for its awe-inspiring standing stones and ancient monuments. One of the best known of these is Lanyon Quoit, a neolithic burial chamber. According to legend, the stone circle known as The Merry Maidens originated when some young girls were turned to stone for dancing on the sabbath. The isolated Men-an-Tol stones may form part of a burial chamber, or a stone circle, or have been used for astrological purposes. On the south coast, the beautiful little cove of almost white sand at Porthcurno is sheltered by jagged granite headlands, and perched on the edge of the cliffs overlooking the cove, is the world famous open-air Minack Theatre, built in the 1930s. One of the most perfect of Cornish fishing coves, Penberth is much loved by artists, and here fishing boats are drawn up alongside the lobster pots and fishing nets. Lamorna Cove has a little harbour with a granite pier from which locally quarried stone was exported in the 18th century. Mousehole, where sturdy stone-built cottages cluster in narrow streets around the snug little harbour, was Cornwall's main fishing port for many years and still provides shelter for small boats.

The Piper standing stone

24 The picturesque fishing village of Mousehole faces east across Mount's Bay

Mousehole harbour

26 The Merry Maidens is a Bronze Age circle of nineteen standing stones

Fishing boats are drawn up on the beach at tiny Penberth Cove

28 Pretty Lamorna Cove has a rocky beach and small quay

The unique Minack Theatre stands in a magical position above the blue waters at Porthcurno

At Porthcurno the granite cliffs contrast with the turquoise waters and dazzling sandy beach

32 The cliffs around Land's End have been eroded into dramatic rock formations

Land's End is England's most westerly point

34 The cliffs at Land's End glow in the late afternoon sun

The solitary Longships Lighthouse is silhouetted against the setting sun

36 Pretty little Sennen Cove lies in a superb setting at the southern end of Whitesand Bay

Sennen Cove

Sennen Cove and Whitesand Bay

40 Sunshine and shadows at Botallack

Old mine engine houses cling precariously to the cliffs at Botallack

The lighthouse at Pendeen Watch dates from 1900 and has a range of 16 nautical miles

44 Perched on the cliff-top near St. Just is the Levant Mine

Gurnard's Head lies in magnificent coastal scenery to the west of Zennor

46 St. Senara's Church at Zennor dates from the 12th century

The historic moorland village of Zennor lies on the road from Land's End to St. Ives

48 Massive Lanyon Quoit is the remains of a long barrow chamber tomb

According to folklore, childhood illnesses could be cured by passing through the Men-an-Tol stone

ST. IVES

Once one of Cornwall's most prosperous ports, exporting fish as far afield as Italy, the harbour is still at the centre of life in St. Ives. Around it is the old town with its cottages clustered together in narrow cobbled streets. Typical of the town's quaint byways, Bunkers Hill was named after the Battle of Bunker Hill which took place during the American War of Independence. Artists have been attracted to St. Ives since the 19th century and the presence of a vibrant artistic community has done much to preserve the character of this ancient fishing port. Now it is internationally known as an artistic centre, and a branch of the Tate Gallery opened here in 1993. It provides a showcase for the best 20th and 21st century art, much of it inspired by this ancient fishing port and its surroundings. Summer visitors enjoy the fine sandy beaches, the mild climate and leisurely walks along this fascinating stretch of coast. Across the bay from St. Ives is Godrevy Point where a dangerous channel which separates the point from Godrevy Island claimed many victims until a lighthouse was built in 1859 to warn sailors away from the savage rocks. The novelist Virginia Woolf knew the area well and it was Godrevy Light which provided the inspiration for her famous novel *To the Lighthouse*.

 St. Ives harbour

Nightfall at St. Ives

St. Ives from the Malakoff

From Cartrew there is a magnificent view across St. Ives Bay to distant Godrevy Island

54 The Tate Gallery houses a superb collection of works by the St. Ives School of Artists

Steep, cobbled Bunkers Hill is typical of old St. Ives

Evening sunshine at St. Ives

58 The harbour at St. Ives is always busy with fishing boats and pleasure craft

The setting sun illuminates the waters of St. Ives Bay

The sands and lighthouse at Godrevy

Godrevy Island
ST. IVES
St. Ives Bay
Zennor
Gurnard's Head
Hayle
Men-an-Tol
Pendeen
Levant Mine
Lanyon Quoit
Botallack
Cape Cornwall
Trengwainton Garden
ST. JUST
Marazion
PENZANCE
St. Michael's Mount
NEWLYN
Trereife Gardens
Trewidden Gardens
Mount's Bay
Whitesand Bay
Praa Sands
Prussia Cove
Rinsey Mine
Mousehole
Sennen Cove
Sennen
Land's End
The Merry Maidens
Lamorna Cove
Penberth
Porthcurno

Penberth Cove

Printed and published by J. Salmon Ltd., 100 London Road, Sevenoaks, Kent.
Telephone: 01732 452381 Email: enquiries@jsalmon.co.uk Website: www.jsalmon.com

ISBN 1 84640 090 2

Photographs by Chris Wormald

Front cover picture: Land's End Back cover picture: Botallack